D1221383

Betty White

THE ILLUSTRATED BIOGRAPHY

By Bill Hewitt
AND THE EDITORS OF LIFE

LIFE ICONS
Managing Editor Robert Sullivan
Director of Photography Barbara Baker Burrows
Deputy Picture Editor Christina Lieberman
Special Contributing Writer Bill Hewitt
Copy Editors Barbara Gogan, Parlan McGaw
Photo Associate Sarah Cates
Consulting Picture Editors Mimi Murphy (Rome), Tala Skari (Paris)

Editorial Director Stephen Koepp
Editorial Operations Director Michael Q. Bullerdick

EDITORIAL OPERATIONS
Richard K. Prue (Director), Brian Fellows (Manager), Richard Shaffer (Production), Keith Aurelio, Charlotte Coco, Tracey Eure, Kevin Hart, Mert Kerimoglu, Rosalie Khan, Patricia Koh, Marco Lau, Brian Mai, Po Fung Ng, Rudi Papiri, Robert Pizarro, Barry Pribula, Clara Renauro, Katy Saunders, Hia Tan, Vaune Trachtman

TIME HOME ENTERTAINMENT
Publisher Jim Childs
Vice President, Business Development & Strategy Steven Sandonato
Executive Director, Marketing Services Carol Pittard
Executive Director, Retail & Special Sales Tom Mifsud
Executive Publishing Director Joy Butts
Director, Bookazine Development & Marketing Laura Adam
Finance Director Glenn Buonocore
Associate Publishing Director Megan Pearlman
Assistant General Counsel Helen Wan
Assistant Director, Special Sales Ilene Schreider
Book Production Manager Suzanne Janso
Design & Prepress Manager Anne-Michelle Gallero
Brand Manager Jonathan White
Associate Prepress Manager Alex Voznesenskiy

Special thanks: Christine Austin, Katherine Barnet, Jeremy Biloon, Susan Chodakiewicz, Rose Cirrincione, Lauren Hall Clark, Jacqueline Fitzgerald, Christine Font, Jenna Goldberg, Hillary Hirsch, David Kahn, Amy Mangus, Robert Marasco, Kimberly Marshall, Amy Migliaccio, Nina Mistry, Roshni Patel, Dave Rozzelle, Ricardo Santiago, Adriana Tierno, Vanessa Wu

Published by LIFE BOOKS, an imprint of
Time Home Entertainment Inc.
135 West 50th Street
New York, New York 10020

ISBN 10: 1-61893-033-8
ISBN 13: 978-1-61893-033-0
Library of Congress Control Number: 2012947632
"LIFE" is a registered trademark of Time Inc.

We welcome your comments and suggestions about LIFE Books. Please write to us at:
LIFE Books
Attention: Book Editors
PO Box 11016
Des Moines, IA 50336-1016

If you would like to order any of our hardcover Collector's Edition books, please call us at 1-800-327-6388. (Monday through Friday, 7:00 a.m.— 8:00 p.m. or Saturday, 7:00 a.m.— 6:00 p.m. Central Time).

PHOTOGRAPHY CREDITS
Page One Globe/Zuma
Title Page Gus Ruelas/Reuters
Contents ©1978 Wallace Seawell/MPTVImages

Produced in association with
KENSINGTON MEDIA GROUP
Editorial Director Morin Bishop
Designer Barbara Chilenskas
Copy Editor Lee Fjordbotten
Fact Checker Ward Calhoun

Introduction 6
New Girl In Town 8
Love is All Around 32
Golden Girl 58
Everybody Loves Betty 76
Just One More 96

Everyone's Sweetheart

THAT WAS THEN, THIS IS NOW
Many moons ago, there were Adam and Eve. More than three decades ago, there were Betty White and Johnny Carson (above). Only yesterday, there were Betty and Slash (above, right), the one-time Guns N' Roses guitarist. While her sidekicks change, Betty goes thrillingly on, as immortal in the public consciousness as Eve herself, but ever Betty, our cherished friend, one of our own.

WE AMERICANS TEND TO CATEGORIZE OR EVEN compartmentalize our celebrities well beyond such overarching designations as Future Star, Star or Superstar; Good Guy, Bad Boy or Party Girl. Sometimes an entertainer, if lucky or talented enough, can transcend a couple or three categories, or grow out of one and into another. An Ingénue or Starlet might become a Serious Actor, before sagging into Has Been once all the "mature" roles have been snapped up by Meryl Streep.

Rarely if ever has one of our constant crop of youthful, lovely, likeable America's Sweethearts found herself at the other end of the career as one of our Beloved Ribald Grandmas. In tracing her unique path, Betty White has, in recent years, entered another and rarefied category: Icon. Mention her name to anyone on the street and there is instant recognition. There is also, just as quickly, a smile.

So many fans who know Betty White don't know enough about her. They see today's white-haired comic who is reliably funny at every turn: in commercials, on talk shows, at roasts, on her sitcom *Hot in Cleveland* or her reality series *Betty White's Off Their Rockers*. They fondly remember her triumph as host of *Saturday Night Live*—she was in just about every skit—and if they are of a certain age, they gladly recall and rehash Rose Nylund's classic scenes on *The Golden Girls*, or Sue Ann Nivens' on *The Mary Tyler Moore Show*.

Some few Whiteheads who have been with Betty a long time seem to recall that she was on just about every game show on TV in the 1960s, and that she hosted the Rose Bowl Parade every year with . . . Who was it? Wasn't it Lorne Greene for many of those years? (It was.)

And wasn't she married to Allen Ludden? (She was.)

But this book goes even farther back, and also goes backstage (and even home) with Betty during the many different chapters of her celebrity. A child of the Midwest, born more than 90 years ago in January 1922, she was still a teenager when she angled for a career in radio, wondering whether to find her way as an on-air personality or what was known during the Big Band Era

LOS ANGELES ZOO/ SPLASH NEWS

as a "girl singer." When television rose to prominence in America's households in the postwar era, she was a pioneer of the new medium, and developed an immense following with her beauty and easy charm on talk shows and game shows. She received her first Emmy nomination in 1951; her most recent would come at age 90 in 2012; in the interim there would be 18 others, and seven wins, in a variety of daytime and nighttime categories. Meanwhile, she would marry twice before finding the love of her life in Ludden, and would give her time to many good causes, particularly those involving the fair treatment of animals.

She would, like Lucille Ball, find her true calling in comedy—and she was always fine with that, and is fine with it still. In recent years, indomitable and unassailable, she has been more than happy to play off-color or against type. She has only grown more popular.

Now then: Who to tell this singular showbiz story? We at LIFE Books had an immediate thought, and we called Bill Hewitt, the longtime *People* magazine writer who knows, or can find, the ins and outs of any subject—crime scene, celebrity scene, any scene. His graceful and fun-filled take on Betty is accompanied by LIFE's characteristic array of wonderful, intimate, always surprising photographs, many of them rarely if ever seen, many of them unpublished for more than half a century.

Betty White is the second in our new series of books, LIFE Icons. The first profile, some of you may know, was of Clint Eastwood. We only wish we were throwing a gala to launch this new line. Clint and Betty out there, cutting a rug during the first dance: That would be something to see.

One thing is for certain. Both of them, and everyone else in the room, would be smiling.

BETTMANN/CORBIS

CHAPTER ONE

NEW GIRL *IN* TOWN

A FRESH-FACED DAUGHTER OF MIDWESTERNERS, SHE WAS READY-MADE FOR TELEVISION. BUT TV WASN'T HAPPENING YET, SO BETTY TUNED HER EAR TO RADIO

DURING THE GREAT DEPRESSION, lovely young women flocking to Southern California in hopes of finding an entrée to show business and stardom were perhaps the only subset of Americans seemingly immune to despair or discouragement. If it is not quite true that 16-year-old Lana (then Judy) Turner was discovered by director Mervyn LeRoy at Schwab's Pharmacy on L.A.'s Sunset Strip in 1937, it *is* cold hard fact that Betty White's big moment came two years later in the same city. For someone whose career has already spanned more than sixty years and counting, Betty's big breakthrough was an episode of almost comical brevity. Fresh out of Beverly Hills High School, she was looking to get her start in radio. The problem was that she wasn't a member of the union, which meant she couldn't perform. Of course the only way to get into the union was to have a job performing—a "Catch-22" if ever there was one, though that phrase would not become part of the vernacular until the 1960s. Betty took to hanging around a producer's office, hoping that she would catch someone's eye. For weeks all she caught were a lot of awkward stares. And then, as they say in Hollywood and elsewhere, lightning struck.

Taking pity on this pretty but inexperienced girl, the producer finally offered to put her in a commercial for a butter substitute called margarine. It was minimal pay, but still an opportunity to get her feet wet and her hands on a union card. All she had to do was utter a single word: "Parkay." Well, she pulled off this feat flawlessly, and the next thing she knew she was a bona fide actress. Perhaps more important, her angel of mercy turned out to be the producer as well of *The Great Gildersleeve*, a phenomenally popular radio program of the day. Soon enough she was doing regular bits on the show. Like Lana Turner, she was on her way.

GLOBE/ZUMA

BEAUTIFUL BETTY
A bombshell in black-and-white, above, Betty is still stunning but more recognizably herself when she sits for the publicity shot (opposite) for her short-lived sitcom *Date with the Angels*.

ALSO LIKE LANA TURNER, WHO HAILED from Idaho, Betty White was not a California girl—not hardly. It is good to pause here for a moment and sketch in some background, because show business was something Betty arrived at more from natural drift than from any carefully charted plan.

ABC PHOTO ARCHIVES/GETTY

SUPERSTOCK/EVERETT

GLOBE/ZUMA (2)

ALL BETTY, ALL THE TIME
Betty is ubiquitous on television in the medium's earliest days, appearing (counterclockwise from right) with movie star Cornel Wilde on one of several iterations of *The Betty White Show*; with beloved co-star Del Moore on *Life with Elizabeth*; and in numerous commercials, like this one, often shot on the set of one of her several shows. *Life with Elizabeth*, one of TV's early situation comedies, ran on Saturday nights and shared the airwaves in the early '50s with *Hollywood on Television*, a talk show—one of the first of its kind as well—that required Betty to banter with her co-host six days a week, five and a half hours a day. If you owned a TV, you became a Betty fan.

She was born on January 17, 1922, in Oak Park, Illinois, and from the very start she had the stamp of the Everywoman. Her given name was just plain Betty, not short for Elizabeth or anything fancier. Her dad, Horace, worked for a lighting company, and her mom, Tess, was a homemaker. An only child, she got the full force of her parents' affection and was to remain close to them throughout their lives.

When Betty was a year and a half old, her dad was transferred to Los Angeles, where the family settled in a modest house. As a child growing up during the Depression, she was fortunate that her dad had a good-paying job. But even then it was tough to make ends meet. To pick up a little extra money, Horace would build radios. As a moneymaking enterprise, however, this wasn't a great success. The reason: Horace, and Tess, too, had a deep love of animals—so much so, that often he would end up swapping his homemade radios for dogs. At one point, Betty later recalled, the family had close to twenty dogs living with them. Thus began her lifelong dedication to animals and their welfare.

Early on, she thought she wanted to be a writer, or perhaps an opera singer. But an appearance in a grammar school play piqued her interest in acting. At her graduation from Beverly Hills High in 1939, she was picked to sing as part of the ceremony. A few weeks later, she and the senior class president were asked to appear in an experiment involving this newfangled technology called television. Decked out in her graduation dress, Betty and her leading man did a truncated version of the operetta *The Merry Widow* in a makeshift studio in a downtown office building. The broadcast didn't air anywhere except for a monitor on the ground floor of the building, where parents and others crowded around to watch.

With the onset of World War II, any hope of making it in show business took a backseat—for Betty and so many others. In her case, though, it was the backseat of a

PX truck, which Betty used to deliver goods like shaving cream to the men stationed at the gun emplacements in hills around Hollywood. (The initial attack at Pearl Harbor had many fearing that California would be the next target.)

Along the way, she picked up a serious boyfriend. Before shipping out overseas, he had given her a ring. For two years they wrote to each other every night. And then they were no more, Betty having crafted one of the infamous Dear John letters that are never fun for anyone. In her memoir *Here We Go Again*, she points out ruefully that she was soon to get her "just desserts" for dumping her beau so unceremoniously. On the rebound, she decided to marry a P-38 pilot, Dick Barker, just before the end of the war. The union was a disaster. She wound up in Belle Center, Ohio, where Barker's parents ran a chicken farm. The thought of slaughtering chickens for a living didn't appeal to her, especially given her feelings about animals. Six months into it, soon after the war came to a conclusion in 1945, the marriage was over, with Betty beating a retreat back to California. "It hurts to fail at something so important," she writes. "And telling yourself it's all part of the learning process doesn't help one damned bit at the time."

By this point, show business was firmly fixed as her ambition. Her strategy was to join a theater group in L.A. The way it worked was that you paid $50 a month for the right to appear in various productions. Again, it was not exactly the path to overnight stardom, but it did get her invaluable experience. Even in those humble circumstances, her natural talent shone through, and she soon emerged as one of the most prominent members of the troupe. It's interesting to note that, unlike most Hollywood aspirants, Betty quite deliberately shunned acting lessons. As she explained to one interviewer, "I just want to bring as much natural as I can. I'm not saying that people who take acting lessons are false. They're much better than I am, but it doesn't work for me."

It was around that time that Betty met an agent and sometime actor named Lane Allan (whose real name was Albert Wooten). He was quickly smitten and wanted to get married. She wasn't so sure and even tried to break things off by disappearing for six weeks on a movie shoot, where she had a bit part and did odd jobs. Upon her return, though, she changed her mind, and in 1947 Betty walked down the aisle for a second time.

If she had managed to get her foot in the door of showbiz, what she hadn't managed to do was to find a way to make a real living. These were tough times for the newlyweds, especially after Lane's agency folded and he had to go to work selling furniture. But Betty didn't panic. Rather than throw away her dreams, she and Lane just tightened their belts and she kept making the rounds.

Once again, fortune smiled on her, or maybe it was fortune that was captivated by *her* glorious smile. Whatever the case, it's worth remembering that the young Betty was a woman of striking looks, with those dimples and that mischievous glint in her eye. So it wasn't so improbable that one day she was approached by a producer with a proposition: Would she be interested in appearing in a television special being hosted by Dick Haynes, a top radio disc jockey in L.A., who was planning to branch out?

Indeed she was interested.

But then came the letdown, sort of: The gig would be unpaid. But think of the exposure! She signed on, and a good thing it was that

ELMER HOLLOWAY/NBC/GETTY

GOING TO THE DOGS

Betty's love of animals goes back a very long way—all the way to Illinois, and following her to California. When a cute, little St. Bernard puppy appeared in a segment of her *Hollywood on Television* show, Betty was immediately smitten, and Stormy (above, several years later and many sizes larger) became a treasured member of Betty's family for the next eleven years.

ABC PHOTO ARCHIVES/GETTY (2)

she did. In this postwar period, L.A.—more swimming pools than television sets, nearly as many Rolls-Royces as swimming pools—was in surf's-up mode, and Betty was in a perfect position to catch the wave. From her gratis gig came a stint on an early game show, a genre she was eventually to conquer in high style (but for now, simply a source of some income). She became better known—a recognizable face. Next, in late 1949, came, as she later put it, "a call that literally changed my life." It was from yet another L.A. disc jockey, Al Jarvis, who was already something of a legend in the entertainment world. He wanted Betty to be his sidekick on a show he was putting together, *Hollywood on Television.*

Despite the clunky long-version title, *H.O.T.*, as it became known, was soon the hottest show around. Suddenly, the talents Jarvis had seen in Betty—her gift for ad lib and easy banter—were on full display. Vital talents they were indeed, because *Hollywood on Television* put enormous demands on its stars. They were on air live for five hours a day, five days a week, with no script and hardly any structure. As Betty put it, "It was like going to television college." Essentially, the format of the show was whatever Jarvis wanted to talk about that day. Sometimes, the topics were serious, such as a crime story in the news that had captured his attention; other times, it was something frivolous. There was a steady stream of celebrity guests—Buster Keaton and Nat King Cole would drop by—and, of course, a slew of commercials to be worked in as seamlessly as possible. Betty's assignment was to keep the conversation flowing, even though she generally had no idea where Jarvis was headed. "No script to fall back on, it was like walking along the edge of a cliff in a high wind," she later wrote. "There was nothing to hang on to but your mental editor. Al and I had to trust each other." For trusting, she was paid $50 a week to start, which seemed a princely sum to Betty at the time; just weeks later, with the show expanding to six days a week and five-and-a-half hours a day, her salary would be raised to $300 a week.

PUSHING THE PRODUCT
In 1957, during the short run of *Date with the Angels*—in the photo above right she is in a makeup session for the show—Betty participates in publicity shots in L.A.'s Griffith Park with guest star Michael Ansara, above left. Ansara is Syrian by ancestry but at the time is starring as Cochise, the Apache chief, on television's *Broken Arrow.*

Audiences loved the show. Alas, husband Lane loved it less. He had visions of a traditional family life, and now he saw his wife being sucked into a career that seemed to occupy all her time. Something had to give, and it did. "He wanted me to stop working," Betty later said. "He didn't want me to be in show business. When you have a calling you have to follow it, so I made the choice, blew the marriage and I've never regretted it."

Lane and Betty separated, though they wouldn't divorce for some time. Betty, on her own again, felt she was in the right place. In this early phase of her career, she had already found the key to her appeal: She brought an agreeable warmth to a cool medium, and, as those endless hours of live broadcast and her ever-rising popularity demonstrated, she was that rare personality who never wore out her welcome. Around this time,

GETTY

Tele-View conducted a poll that confirmed that impression. It found that Betty was "the female personality viewers would most like to invite into their homes." By the 21st century, once those polls had evolved into the hyper-scientific, ultra-sophisticated "Q ratings," Betty would still be at the top, sharing the annual best-liked-actor title with Tom Hanks.

She was no longer anyone's second banana. Ripe for stardom was more like it. Now in her late twenties, she saw opportunity at every turn. While still doing *Hollywood on Television*, she launched her own series, *The Betty White Show*, a variety program that aired on Sunday evenings. Then there was *Life with Elizabeth*, an early sitcom in which she played a suburban housewife, which earned Betty her first Emmy nomination, in 1951. That was followed by another incarnation of *The Betty White Show*, the second of three—so far. (Who knows what the future holds?)

There would be several more television programs—quiz shows, comedies, TV movies—as well as a few bumps in the road and a host more awards. But, as the World War II generation was about to grow older and their baby boomers were about to grow up, the deal was already sealed: They would grow along with Betty White (and then, so would the grandkids).

TOP OF THE HEAP
By the end of the 1950s, Betty is a legitimate fixture on TV, having been on the air almost continuously since 1949—barely a year after the inception of genuine network television in the United States.

New Girl In Town

Trial By Fire

Betty began co-hosting *Hollywood on Television* in 1949 with Al Jarvis, an already established star on radio and a man to whom Betty has expressed a deep debt of gratitude for all he taught her about handling the demands of a daily, live, largely ad-libbed talk show as well as negotiating the perils of her own growing celebrity. In 1952, Jarvis left the show for another project, and a new host was introduced, young Hollywood star Eddie Albert (right, with Betty, left). Arnold became one of Betty's lifetime friends but left the show after just six months when Hollywood came calling with an offer he couldn't refuse, starring opposite Gregory Peck and Audrey Hepburn in the classic film *Roman Holiday*. After his departure, Betty would briefly take on the role of the show's sole host, before the program was shut down in 1953. Betty would miss her many friends associated with the show, but not those 30-plus hours a week of live television.

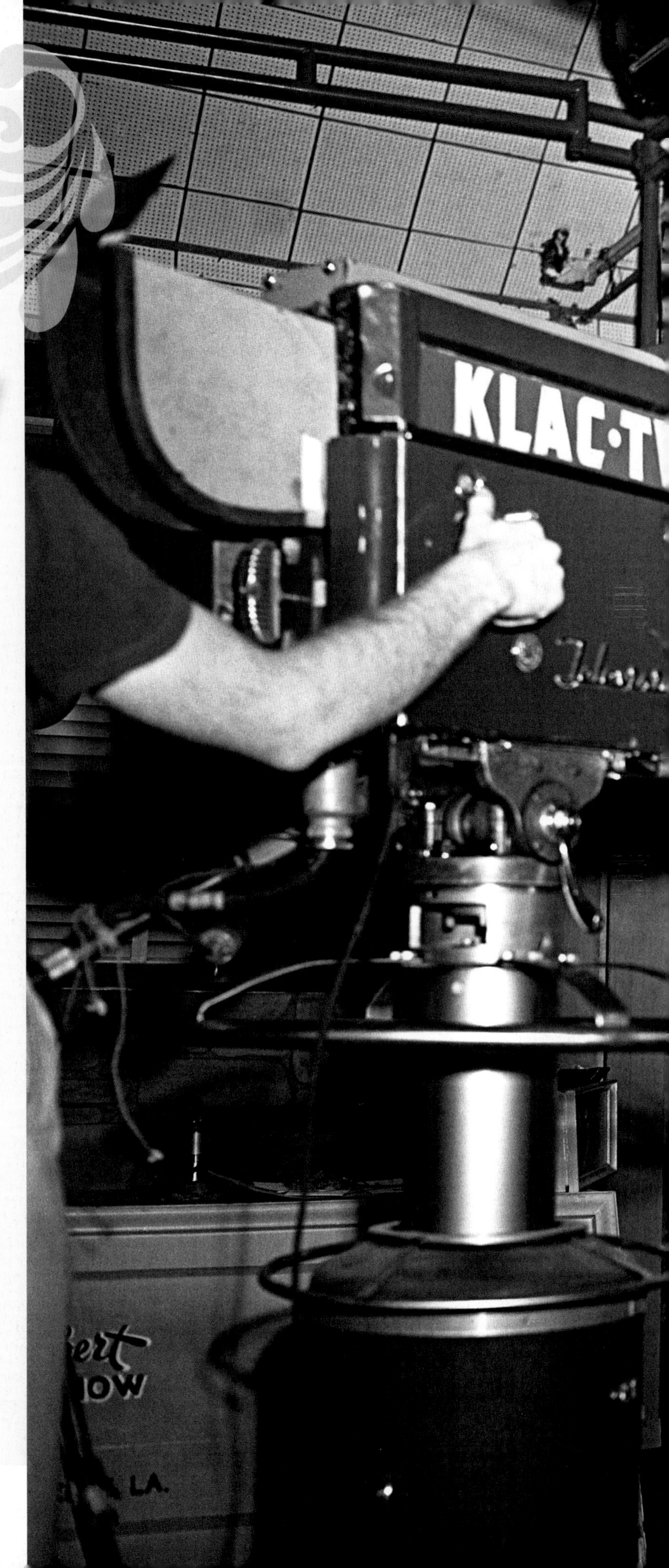

NIGEL DOBINSON/HULTON/GETTY

Comic Gold

Life with Elizabeth, which ran from 1952 to 1955, gave the public an early taste of Betty's knack for comedy. At left she hams it up for the audience; at right she is featured in a scene with a lovable pair of St. Bernards. Her deft comedic talents will be largely forgotten for a decade and a half, between the demise of her sitcom *Date with the Angels* and her appearance on *The Mary Tyler Moore Show* in 1973. For its first two seasons, *Life with Elizabeth* was performed live in front of a studio audience, a much more comfortable situation from Betty's point of view than shooting the show on tape, which became necessary after the program was syndicated in 1953. With no audience to guide them, she and co-star Del Moore had to guess at the right moments and just how long to pause for laughs, a dilemma she later described as "a little like doing comedy in a mortuary." Still, the show prospered and survived two more seasons.

Funny Face (overleaf)

When Betty went national on NBC in 1954, the publicity machine went into high gear, promoting Betty's wonderfully expressive face and highly likable personality. The promotional copy that accompanied these publicity shots included this: "Betty White's smile comes naturally. So do the quizzical expression and the unaffected facial gestures. So she's the Cinderella girl-next-door on NBC's coast-to-coast TV show—chatting, singing and always friendly."

PHOTOFEST (2)

BETTMANN/CORBIS (2)

NBC/PHOTOFEST (2)

Network News

While her work on *Hollywood on Television*, which was broadcast on KLAC-TV in Los Angeles, made Betty famous on the West Coast, it was not until *Life with Elizabeth* was syndicated in 1953 that the rest of the country came to learn who Betty was. Her national profile took an even greater leap with the second *Betty White Show*, which aired nationally on NBC in 1954. (Betty shows her enthusiasm for this development on the opposite page.) The daytime talk show included similar features to those on *Hollywood on Television*, including a focus on animals. (Betty appears above with animal trainer Larry White and a five-year-old elephant guest.) While earning excellent ratings in its original time slot at noon, the show fell prey to network meddling—the geniuses in charge switched her time slot twice—and the program was replaced by Tennessee Ernie Ford after the show's final broadcast at the end of the year. Betty was distraught, but her career was far from over.

KNBH
NBC
RCA

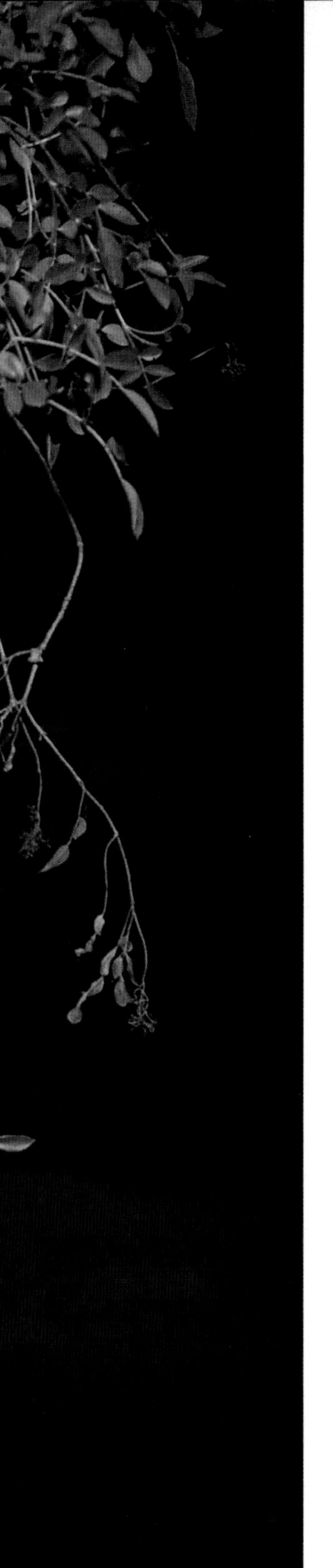

GLOBE/ZUMA

"Animals Don't Lie."

Whether in a Western-themed publicity shot with a horse (left) or a scene with a chimp from her sitcom *Date with the Angels* in 1957 (right, bottom) or at home with her beloved Pekingese, Bandit (top), in 1954, Betty has always been more than happy to share her life—on camera or at home—with her many animal friends. (She once admitted to Barbara Walters that she prefers animals to humans. As she noted in her recent book, *If You Ask Me*, "Can you blame me? Animals don't lie. Animals don't criticize. If animals have moody days, they handle them better than humans do.") Bandit even lent his name to Betty's first production company, Bandy Productions, formed on a handshake with writer George Tibbles and KLAC station manager Don Fedderson.

HERB BALL/NBC/GETTY

ABC PHOTO ARCHIVES/GETTY

HULTON/GETTY

Briefly in Limbo

After the cancellation of *The Betty White Show* at the end of 1954, Betty was feeling a bit at sea, with two failed marriages and several now-ended television projects behind her. But Betty was never one for self-pity, and her first appearance as host of the Tournament of Roses Parade in January 1955, as well as photo shoots like the one above, taken at her home in 1956, keep her in the public eye. Meanwhile, her creative team is working on a new sitcom, and soon producer Don Fedderson has found a sponsor—Plymouth—for the new show and a network—ABC—to air it. By 1957, Betty is ready for a triumphal trip to New York, opposite, for a press event promoting this latest offering, *Date with the Angels*.

ABC PHOTO ARCHIVES/GETTY

FLIGHT
708
NES

GLOBE /ZUMA

Not a Great Date

Begun with the best of intentions, *Date with the Angels* proves to be an unhappy experience for Betty—"I think I can honestly say that that was the only time I have ever wanted to get out of a show," she would write later—though it does give her additional national exposure, and yields fetching stills like the one at left, associated with a "sailing" episode. The biggest problem is her co-star, Bill Williams (lifting Betty off her feet, above), who "simply didn't think 'funny,'" as Betty writes in *Here We Go Again*; Williams lacked the bounteous comic instincts of her *Life with Elizabeth* co-star, Del Moore. The show, in its original form, lasted less than a single season. Typical of Betty, she will nonetheless remain good friends with Bill and his wife, Barbara Hale, who played Raymond Burr's secretary, Della Street, on *Perry Mason*.

ABC PHOTO ARCHIVES/GETTY

At a Crossroads

As the '50s draw to a close, with ten years under her belt as the host of two daytime talk shows and the star of two sitcoms, Betty's television career is well established. But what would be her next step? As she would write later, she was soon "out of drawers and closets to clean." Would glamour shots, like these two, taken in 1958, suggest a new direction for her as a leading lady? Or would her late 30s take her in yet another direction? The answer to these—and all—questions lay waiting across the continent, in New York City.

CHAPTER TWO

LOVE IS *ALL* AROUND

EVEN BEFORE THE MARY TYLER MOORE SHOW *ARRIVED, EVERYTHING—THE PERSONAL AS WELL AS PROFESSIONAL—WAS COMING UP ROSES FOR BETTY*

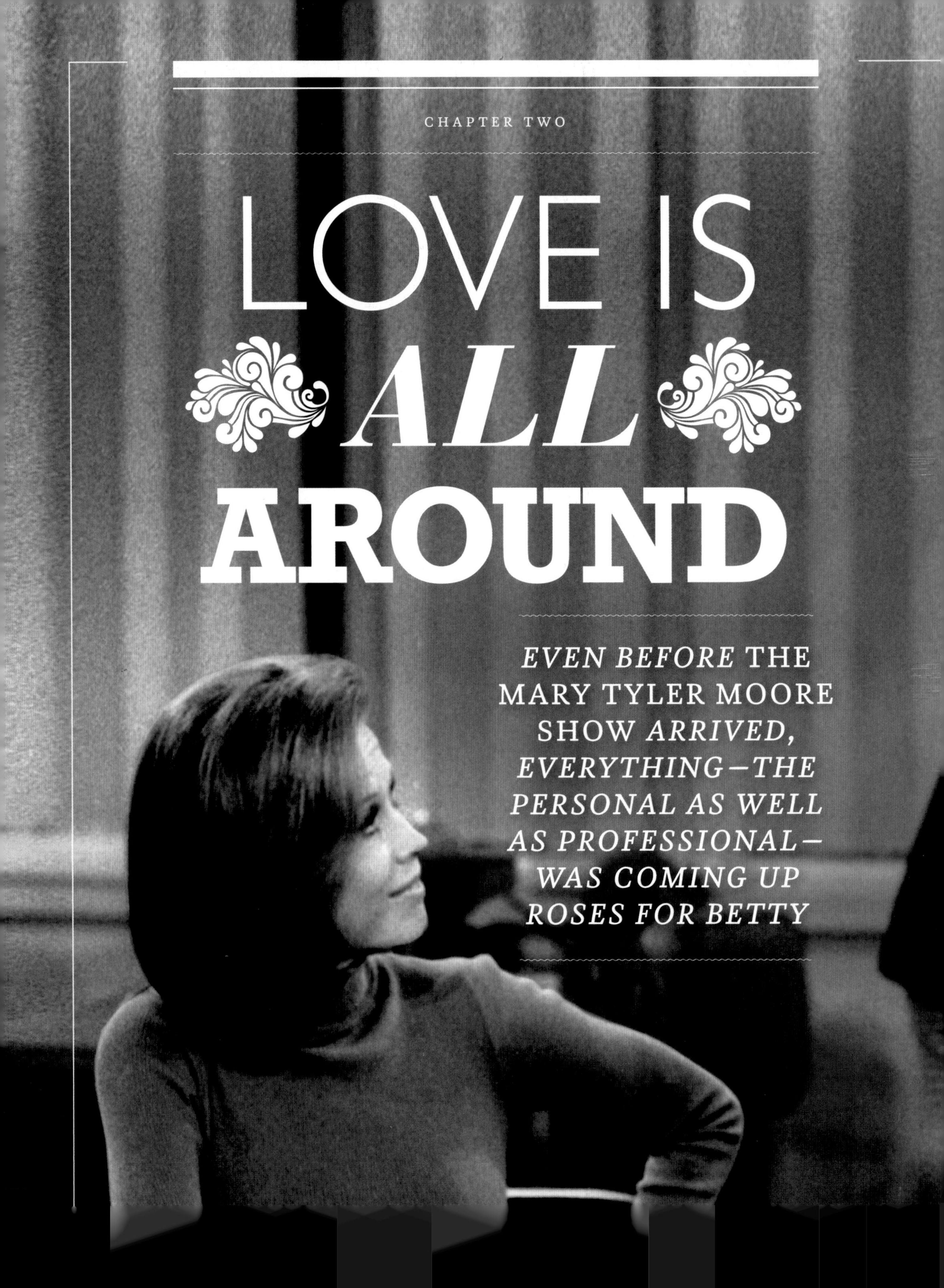

EVERETT

THE TELEVISION OF THE 1950s seems light-years away from the entertainment extravaganza we've come to expect on today's small screens. Back in the day, there were touchstones—one place in the morning for people to gather, one or two trusted news shows later in the day and the *Tonight Show* at bedtime. Today there are countless shows 24/7, not to mention all the other media continuously blasting out of computers and cell phones. One of the constants, though, has been Betty White. America loved her then and wanted as much of her as it could get. The same is still true.

A PAIR OF LONG-RUNNING HITS
Two constants in Betty's life in the '60s and '70s are her presence at the annual Tournament of Roses Parade, which she began hosting in 1955—she is shown below at the 1970 parade—and, of course, her marriage to Allen Ludden (opposite, with Betty on the *Password* set in1963, the year they were wed). Of her decision to finally accept the last of Allen's insistent proposals, she would later write, "The choices were suddenly very clear and very narrow: stay in California and spend the rest of my life watching this man on television, knowing what I had lost, or . . . When the phone rang that evening I didn't say, 'Hello.' I said, 'YES!' " It was a decision she would never regret.

Of course, there was one other TV truism then as now: You could always be cancelled, often through no fault of your own. And Betty was, right off the bat. The second *Betty White Show*, for instance, ran only one season, despite putting up decent numbers. When she was called to New York at the end of 1954 and told of the show being terminated, she was crushed. "I thought it was the end of the world," she later recalled, "that I was never going to work again, that I was just going to walk into the Atlantic Ocean and never come up."

EVERETT

Nothing so dramatic took place, of course, and any self-doubt was wildly misplaced. Betty was still omnipresent on the tube. Among other things, she landed the plum assignment of hosting the annual Tournament of Roses (Rose Bowl) Parade, a job she was to hold for 20 years, becoming, along with pardner Lorne Greene, something of an icon. She was good at this gig; standing around gabbing came as naturally to her as breathing: "I'm a big talker. If I don't have anything to say, I say it anyway."

This loquaciousness and bright, sometimes devilish, sense of humor made her a favorite of the talk show format that was beginning to catch on in the '50s. She became a regular on Jack Paar's *Tonight Show*, appearing more than 70 times, and then on Johnny Carson's version as well. But what really kept her in the public eye was the rise of game shows, which were as ubiquitous in that era as reality TV is in our own. Betty was especially pleased to appear on them for the simple reason that she really, really liked them. As a child in the Midwest, she had delighted in making up games with her parents. "We'd sit around the breakfast table or driving on vacation and we'd play games," she said. "It was like gamblers who bet on anything. We could make a game out of anything." She retained her enthusiasm.

The roster of shows she was featured on—*I've Got a Secret, To Tell the Truth, What's My Line?*—offers a time capsule of the era. Fortunately, Betty was never touched by the quiz show scandal of the '50s, which uncovered the dirty truth that certain contestants—the

GABI RONA/MPTV IMAGES

THE GAME'S THE THING
Betty appeared in a cavalcade of game shows in the '60s and '70s, including *To Tell the Truth, I've Got a Secret, Liar's Club, Password* (of course), *What's My Line?* and *The Match Game*. Above, Betty is pictured with fellow actor and good friend Pat O'Brien, who would later be Betty's next-door neighbor in Brentwood, California.

telegenic ones, mostly—had been given the answers ahead of time. The crooks behind the scandal might have been able to bribe the kids, but no one would dare to try to corrupt the young actress who was regularly referred to as America's sweetheart.

BETTY'S IMMERSION IN THE WORLD OF game shows proved to be a turning point not only for her career, but also for her personal life. For several years she had been happily involved in a long-distance relationship with a man named Phil Cochran, whom she had met one night when he was a fellow guest on Jack Paar's show. Dashing and handsome, Cochran was a remarkable guy. During World War II, he had been an ace fighter pilot in the Burma-India theater, where his derring-do became the stuff of legend. The cartoonist Milton Caniff based characters in his comic strips *Terry and the Pirates* and *Steve Canyon* on Colonel Cochran. The meeting on the Paar set led to a serious romance. Cochran proposed marriage, but Betty declined. She simply couldn't leave California and move to Erie, Pennsylvania, where Cochran owned a trucking company. Nevertheless they were able to see each other regularly, thanks in part to Betty's visits to New York for game show or talk show gigs.

Enter Allen Ludden to upend the arrangement.

Allen, who had been a brainy guy at the University of Texas, was what could be called a charismatic nerd. His first claim to fame after graduation was as the host of the *G.E. College Bowl*, a game show that pitted university students against each other. The show became a huge hit, and Ludden became a household name.

In October 1961, Ludden became the host of *Password*, in which celebrities teamed with ordinary contestants, the goal being to get the partner to guess a password by the use of one-word clues—a version of charades at one remove. Betty appeared on the show when it was less than a month old. She knew of Allen and had seen him many times on *G.E. College Bowl*. What she did not know was that his wife, Margaret, was dying of cancer. Despite the personal anguish caused by Margaret's condition, Allen had continued working. As it happened, the week that Betty appeared on *Password* was the same week that Margaret passed away, leaving Allen and their three young children bereft.

By chance (or maybe not), a few months later Betty and Allen's respective agents booked them to perform together in summer stock on Cape Cod. "Somehow, we were instant friends," she recalled later. After a few weeks Allen began greeting her with a startling salutation, "Will you marry me?"

She remembered: "Well, it was a joke and I laughed it off, and he'd laugh it off."

Or was it a joke?

The play in which they were performing, *Critic's Choice*, called for them to share a long kiss at the end. One night, Phil Cochran, who was visiting, thought he detected more than professionalism in that kiss. When he mentioned his concerns to Betty, she said he was being silly. They were just actors playing the roles, right? Later, she was to credit her former beau with greater insight than she herself had possessed: "I guess he knew I was attracted to Allen long before I did."

Over the next year, Allen turned up the pressure with his marriage proposals. "Finally, it wasn't a joke anymore," Betty said later. "I said, 'No, no way.' So, he bought a wedding

ring, a beautiful gold wedding ring with diamonds all around it. One night at dinner he gave it to me and said, 'You might as well take it, because you're going to put it on one day.' " Even then she demurred. As was the case in her relationship with Phil Cochran, her reluctance stemmed from her desire to stay in California rather than move to the New York area, where Allen lived. But Allen—also a World War II veteran (he had been awarded a Bronze Star) and evidently more resolute than Cochran—was not a man to be thwarted when on a mission. He took the ring and put it on a chain that he wore around his neck. That way, every time he took off his shirt, at the beach or wherever, the ring would be staring at Betty like a hypnotic pendant. Or at least, that seemed to be Allen's general idea.

Allen eventually hit on a plan that would surely melt Betty's obdurate refusals. At Easter he sent her a toy bunny with diamond, ruby and sapphire earrings. That night when he called, she finally said yes. Later, she said, he teased her that she had married him "not for the earrings, but for the stuffed bunny." And she joked right back that the real reason she acquiesced was that she adored Allen's two poodle puppies and couldn't bear the thought of life without them.

Despite all her prior hemming and hawing, Betty quickly settled into married life, which was a good thing, because her new situation in Chappaqua, New York, came complete with a ready-made family: Allen's children, David, 14, Martha, 13, and Sarah, 10. From the first, she had embraced the kids, and they her. But

BETTY'S LABOR OF LOVE

The Pet Set, perhaps Betty's favorite project of her long career, sadly ran only one season (39 episodes in those days) but it did lead her to the Morris Animal Foundation, a charity that she has been associated with ever since. In the picture above, Betty is shown with Beverly Garland, then starring as Fred MacMurray's second wife on the hit sitcom, *My Three Sons*.

she and Allen would never have offspring of their own, which was how she wanted it. "I made a very conscious decision not to have children, which was rather unheard of at that time," she told a reporter in 1986. "I love children, and if there are kids around, we all migrate together, then I go home and they go home, which is fine with me. I just didn't feel that it would be fair to try to make a split between my life and my career."

Looking back, did she have any second thoughts? "Everybody said, 'Oh, when you get down the line, you're going to regret not having had children.' I never have. I haven't regretted it for a minute."

EVERETT

CAREER MAKEOVER

By the time this photograph was taken in 1977, Betty had become a fixture on *The Mary Tyler Moore Show*, having won two Emmy Awards (1975 and '76) and been nominated for a third, for her uproarious portrayal of Sue Ann Nivens. No longer seen by most Americans as simply a clever game-show contestant, Betty was now recognized for what she has since unquestionably become: one of America's most gifted comic actresses.

Her relationship with Ludden brought with it a new circle of friends. For instance, Allen was close to novelist John Steinbeck and his wife, Elaine, having met Elaine at the University of Texas. A first visit to the Steinbeck apartment left a lasting impression on Betty. "It was hard not to be a little in awe of John at first," she wrote in her memoir *Here We Go Again*. "It didn't help my state of nerves that at the moment we walked in, John was scratching out his acceptance speech for the Nobel Prize." Steinbeck later presented Allen and Betty with that draft of the speech, which Betty proudly displayed in their home.

Allen's closest pal was Grant Tinker, a major producer and all-around Hollywood power broker. Tinker was married to Mary Tyler Moore, then a rising television star, thanks to her role on *The Dick Van Dyke Show*. In the years to come, the two couples would become extremely close. The four of them even shared a memorable vacation together in Bora Bora. In the early years of their close friendship, Betty and Mary had no way of knowing that they would share some television magic only a few years down the road.

No sooner had Betty grown accustomed to living on the East Coast than it became clear that L.A. was where Allen, too, needed to be in order to forward his television career. They moved west in 1968. Betty had been appearing steadily on game shows and the like, but shortly the opportunity arose to host what she regarded as her "dream show." It was called *The Pet Set*. On each episode, a celebrity would bring his or her pet to the studio for what might be called a canine klatch (never a cat fight), and then there would be a segment involving some exotic wild animal or another. Betty's favorite "guest" was a Bengal tiger named Sultan. "It was," she later said, "the happiest I've ever been on television." That assessment is particularly striking in light of what was to come.

There are a number of natural misconceptions about Betty's career-shaping role on *The Mary Tyler Moore Show*. The first is the assumption that she got the part because of her friendship with Mary, or Allen's friendship with Tinker. Not true. As it happens, it wasn't until the fourth season that the producers came up with the idea of adding a character they liked to refer to as "a Betty White–type"—in this case, a strenuously cheery but half-baked cooking maven who did segments on the show's fictional TV station, WJM. Even then, it took them a few days to get around to the notion that, *Hey, maybe the real Betty would be perfect for the part.* "They couldn't find anyone sickening enough," she joked. So, without consulting Mary, the producers hired her for the part.

The other odd thing, in retrospect, was how limited the role was, but how much mileage Betty got out of it. As Sue Ann Nivens, The Happy Homemaker, a saccharine presence on camera but a bloodcurdling witch off—not to mention a nymphomaniac who in one episode managed the neat trick of bedding Lars, the unseen husband of Mary's close friend Phyllis—she created a character for the ages. Memorable. But now, test your memory, and take a guess at how many episodes Sue Ann appeared in, out of the

MPTV IMAGES

show's total of 168. Eighty? Sixty? Try 44. Looking back, you marvel that the producers intuitively knew that Sue Ann was a dish that should be served sparingly.

Betty has always been modest: "The magic was in the writing," she said. But everyone, including Betty, realized that she had been reborn as an actress, and she took home two Emmys for her portrayal of Sue Ann. "Everybody was so surprised," she recalled. " 'Why, she can act! Isn't that amazing?' It really did turn my career completely around."

If her acting prowess was a bit surprising to some, Betty's willingness—even eagerness—to play against image was even more so. Let's face it, nobody can believe, or wants to believe, that anyone can be as perfect as "Betty White." Somewhere in each of us there lurks the secret desire for the naughty side. Betty the actress was more than willing to offer that perspective on herself, and to do so with wicked relish. Of course, the real joke may have been on us, for thinking that Betty or anyone was so pure in the first place. Later, she liked to tell a joke about how, when Allen was asked by people whether there was any similarity between his real-life wife and the fictional Sue Ann, he liked to crack that they were very much alike, "except Betty can't cook."

Somewhat unexpectedly, Mary decided to end her show after the 1977 season. Betty felt that there were still a couple of good years left in the cast, but Mary wanted to pursue her love of dance, and that was that. The classic program and several classic portrayals—Mary's own, Ed Asner's Lou Grant, Ted Knight's Ted Baxter, Gavin MacLeod's Murray Slaughter, and Betty's Sue Ann—were put to rest. (Asner's would resurface in a spinoff.)

Betty, 55 years old, now on top in so many ways old and new, looked to the always mercurial but, in her case, usually kind fates and wondered, *What's next?*

A CAST FOR THE AGES

The unforgettable *Mary Tyler Moore Show* regulars, clockwise from lower left: Betty as Sue Ann Nivens, Gavin MacLeod as soft-hearted news writer Murray Slaughter, Ed Asner as crusty news director Lou Grant, Ted Knight as bumbling anchorman Ted Baxter, Georgia Engel as Ted's dimwitted girlfriend (later wife) Georgette and Mary Tyler Moore as Mary Richards, the show's grounded center.

"LOCKSMITH
"APPEAL"
"BACKFIRE"
"BLAB"
"ADMIT"
"CAMPHOR"
OBEY"
"MOTTO"
"MEDDLE"

Love Is All Around

CBS/GETTY

Winner and Still Champion

With her sitcom days seemingly behind her, Betty found career salvation in the rising tide of game shows and late-night talk that was beginning to flood the airwaves in the '60s. A budding friendship with Mark Goodson, the creative force behind many of the most successful game shows of the era, as well as her marriage to host extraordinaire Allen Ludden, established her as the belle of the game circuit, while her many appearances on Jack Paar's *Tonight Show* made her a familar face to the insomniac set as well. Betty loved Allen's show, *Password,* and was exceptionally adept at coming up with just the right one-word clues to induce her non-celebrity playing partners to guess the right answer. Above, she celebrates one of her many *Password* wins; opposite, she poses with Allen and frequent celebrity contestant Jim Backus, best remembered as the aristocratic Thurston Howell III on *Gilligan's Island*.

EVERETT

EVERETT (3)

Fun and Games

Quiz shows of every stripe proliferated in the '60s. There were intellectually challenging ones, like *You Don't Say* (opposite, Betty appears on the show with Lorne Greene, the paterfamilias of the Cartwright clan on the enormously popular *Bonanza*), a charades-type exercise in which celebrity partners try to guess popular names or characters by breaking answers into sound-alike syllables. On *It's Your Bet*, one half of a celebrity couple like Ludden and White (right) listens to a question by telephone and attempts to predict how the spouse will respond. Then there was considerably less testing fare like *The Match Game*, one of the most enduring shows of the era, which morphed over the years from a traditional word quiz to quite a risqué enterprise, with contestants finishing such phrases as, "Did you catch a glimpse of that girl on the corner? She has the world's biggest _______." Jovial host Gene Rayburn, at top with (clockwise from upper left) Ludden, Brett Somers, Charles Nelson Reilly, Betty, Richard Dawson and Dolly Martin, presides over the shenanigans with great good humor.

GLOBE/ZUMA

Passing Parades

Betty co-hosted the Tournament of Roses Parade for 20 years, including 19 for NBC and a single final year for CBS. (At left, she poses for a publicity shot for the event.) Over the years, her co-hosts included everyone from John Forsythe to Bill Cullen to Raymond Burr to one disastrous year with Arthur Godfrey, who insisted on not preparing and then commenting continuously on sights during the parade that were not being shown on camera. Over the years, her preparation for the event became more extensive and time-consuming, involving travel to Pasadena several days early and numerous interviews with the float builders and others associated with the parade. Eventually she teamed up with Lorne Greene for several Rose Bowl parades as well as for ten broadcasts of the annual Macy's Thanksgiving Day Parade in New York City (opposite). She would later write of her many parade broadcasts: "It got so that if I saw a line of cars waiting for a signal, I had to fight the urge to do a commentary."

NBC/GETTY

Domestic Bliss

When Betty finally accepted his marriage proposal, Allen had no vacation time available from *Password* and a marriage license in California required a three-day waiting period for a blood test. So the bride and groom flew with Betty's parents to Las Vegas, which had no such requirement, and were married (above) on June 14, 1963, by David Zenoff, the same judge who had tied the knot for Grant Tinker and Mary Tyler Moore in 1962. After a long weekend in Laguna Beach, California, that passed for a honeymoon, Allen was back at work on *Password*, with Betty as a contestant on the first show after their wedding. While Betty and Allen had initially planned to make some renovations to the home in Briarcliff Manor, New York, where Allen had been living with his three children, they soon heard of a wonderful opportunity in nearby Chappaqua that combined an 18th-century farmhouse and barn. The couple instantly fell in love with the place (right), which included a swimming pool, ancient stone walls and acres and acres of old apple orchards. The entire clan would live there happily until circumstances dictated a move back to California in 1968.

GLOBE/ZUMA (2)

GLOBE/ZUMA

One Big, Happy Family

After the wedding, the Ludden kids (clockwise from Betty's right, Sarah, David and Martha) took to Betty immediately. In fact, they were already fans, having become very close with her during the summer of 1962, when Allen and Betty performed together in *Critic's Choice* on Cape Cod, in Dennis, Masscahusetts, and then had a wonderful, warm Thanksgiving together the following November. They even participated in and encouraged their father in his "campaign" to persuade Betty to marry him, happily tabulating "check points" every time Allen or Betty said something positive to one another. So when she finally said "yes," they were almost as thrilled as Allen was and happily settled into their new Chappaqua home along with their poodles, Emma and Willie. Given the couple's predilections, it is no surprise that the house was filled with games, including a running gin rummy contest between Allen and Betty (opposite)—she claimed to be the consistent winner.

BOB WANDS/AP

Betty's Favorite Show

Betty's single season of *The Pet Set* was among the most enjoyable of her life as she hosted a parade of celebrities and their favorite pets. Counterclockwise from opposite: Crooner Johnny Mathis drops by with his English Sheepdog, Henry; Bob Barker, of *Price Is Right* fame, visits with his bassett hound, Mr. Rubbard; and young hunk James Brolin, right, then starring in *Marcus Welby, M.D.* with Robert Young, is on the show with Buck, a huge harlequin Great Dane, which

EVERETT

is sort of a cross between a traditional Great Dane and a Dalmatian. In every episode of *The Pet Set*, Betty would craft the theme of the show around the guest. So the appearance by Brolin, for example, was followed by a filmed segment from his ranch that featured his striking Appaloosa horses. Other visitors included Lorne Greene and his German shepherds; Mike Connors, the star of *Mannix*, and his black Labrador retriever; Mary Tyler Moore and her two poodles, Diswilliam and Maude; and on and on. Betty enjoyed every minute. Sadly, at the end of the season, Carnation, which had been the major sponsor of the show, made a decision to reallocate its advertising away from programming like Betty's show. *Pet Set* was no more, but Betty's passion for animals would endure.

GABI RONA/MPTVIMAGES

Those '70s Shows

In addition to her star turn on *The Mary Tyler Moore Show* (see following pages), the '70s saw Betty appearing all around the TV dial in pretty much every format the medium offered. She continued to work the game show circuit—during the decade she appeared 20 times on *Password All-Stars*, four times on *You Don't Say*, twice on *The Cross-Wits*, three times on *Hollywood Squares*, seven times on *Password Plus* and 11 times on *Match Game*. She continued to appear regularly on the talk shows—twice on *The Merv Griffin Show*, once on *The Mike Douglas Show*, three times on Johnny Carson's *Tonight Show* and four times on Dinah Shore's show, *Dinah!* But with her success on *Mary Tyler Moore*, she was perhaps in greatest demand for her talents as a comic actress. Well-received appearances on *The Carol Burnett Show* (of her invitation from Carol, she would later write: "I was thrilled beyond words. It had never occurred to me that I would ever get a chance to go over and play with those crazy, gifted people.") opened the door to a wave of new variety shows and Betty walked right in, making people laugh in 1974 on the popular *Sonny and Cher Show* (top, with from left, Ken Berry, Sonny, Cher and Flip Wilson); in 1976 on the less popular *Cos* (above, with from left, Arte Johnson and Bill Cosby); and in 1977 on *The Jacksons* (opposite, with from left, La Toya, Janet and Rebbie Jackson). Was there a harder working woman in show business than Betty White?

EVERETT (2)

Comedienne Extraordinaire

As close friends of Mary Tyler Moore and Grant Tinker—the star and producer, respectively, of *The Mary Tyler Moore Show*—Betty and Allen had closely monitored the creation and early stages of the show in 1970, hoping against hope that their friends' new project would be successful in the dog-eat-dog world of network television. As Betty writes in *Here We Go Again:* "We sweated out revisions before it went on the air and revisions after. . . . That first season, it was thrilling to watch the show's initial shaky baby steps become steadier and see it gradually begin to run." By the time the fourth season rolled around, the show was a bona fide hit, regularly earning a raft of Emmy nominations every year. So it was a surprise when Betty received a call from Allan Burns, one of the co-creators of the show, asking her to appear in the role of Sue Ann Nivens. Although the part had called for a "Betty White–type" there had been some concern at the show that Betty's friendship with Mary might create awkwardness if things did not go well. In the end, such fears were cast aside and Betty White took the "Betty White" part herself. Mary, who suprisingly enough had not been consulted, was ecstatic when she heard of the decision, though she facetiously told Betty, "Oh no you don't! I may not butt into the show often, but I *do* have veto power!" The character, saccharine sweet but sexually voracious—particularly in her ceaseless attempts to seduce Ed Asner's Lou Grant (opposite)—was instantly popular. Betty credits Mary with Sue Ann's success: "No matter how funny the part is, if a *guest* character is someone the *lead* character doesn't like, the audience can often get protective and not respond well to the newcomer. . . . It was thanks to Mary's choice as an actress that Sue Ann worked. Rather than disliking her, Mary Richards found Sue Ann laughable, so the audience could relax and laugh with her." Ultimately, audiences and critics alike came to embrace Betty (right, with Mary and Ed) and her alter ego, Sue Ann. Betty would walk away with two Emmys for the role, in 1975 and '76 (top). Her career as a comic actress was resurrected—forevermore.

ON THE AIR

BETTMANN/CORBIS

CBS/GETTY

Going Out on Top

Since Mary had informed the cast that the 1976–77 season would be the show's last, there was an elegiac, bittersweet quality to the entire year. Mary's decision was certainly not based on the show's standing with the public—it continued to be a hit and had earned the Emmy as oustanding comedy series in 1976, as it would in '77 after that final season. She just had other fish to fry, most notable a burning desire to use her dancing talents more extensively. (Sadly, Mary has never had another successful television program, nor was she ever able to parlay her dancing abilities into a succesful vehicle for her. She did go on, however, to establish her serious acting credentials with her role as the brittle mother in 1980's *Ordinary People*, for which she received an Academy Award nomination.) Even with excitement high about future projects—Ed Asner would reprise his *MTM* role in the drama, *Lou Grant*; Cloris Leachman would star in the spin-off *Phyllis*, based on her character in the show; Betty would front a short-lived fourth iteration of *The Betty White Show*—the cast was acutely aware of the once-in-a-lifetime experience they were leaving behind. "When the last week arrived and we gathered as always on Monday morning, the atmosphere was so tangible you could almost see it in the air," Betty writes in *Here We Go Again*. "We didn't really discuss it, we all just hung out together. . . . The last scene we read through only once on Thursday, then blocked it Friday just in time for dress and show. Do you know the feeling when you try and talk but the corners of your mouth keep pulling down and you know you're losing it? By showtime, however, we had ourselves pretty much in hand. . . . We even made it into the final scene [left and above] with flying colors. It was not until Ed, as Lou Grant, said, 'I treasure you people!' that everything went to hell in a handbasket. . . . We knew we would all still see each other. We knew no one had died. But something very precious would never be again." The audience felt precisely the same way: Was there a viewer in America who did not fight tears while watching Mary turn out the lights in the WJM newsroom for the very last time?

CHAPTER THREE

GOLDEN GIRL

BETTY LOST THE LOVE OF HER LIFE WHEN CANCER FELLED HUSBAND ALLEN LUDDEN BUT, AS USUAL, WORK HELPED FILL THE VOID AND SOON SHE WAS BASKING IN THE GLOW OF ANOTHER HIT SERIES

DESPITE TWO SHORT-LIVED marriages, Betty had enjoyed a 40-year run of professional good fortune, and now, with Allen Ludden, she was entered upon a period of personal as well as professional well-being. But the next phase of her life was to be marked by anguish. In 1980, Allen fell ill. At first, the situation didn't seem all that serious: a persistent fever and some fatigue. Visits to the doctor didn't turn up anything initially; he'd get better, he'd surely get better. But eventually a scan showed something in his stomach. He underwent surgery, and the news wasn't good. It was cancer, and the surgeons had not been able to get all of it..

FAB FOUR
From the time she read the first script and learned that Jay Sandrich, who had directed most of *The Mary Tyler Moore Show* episodes, would direct the pilot, Betty was very interested in *The Golden Girls*. With a quartet of seasoned performers like (clockwise from right, opposite) Betty, Bea Arthur, Estelle Getty and Rue McClanahan, and exceptionally sharp and clever writing, the show began with enormous advantages. "We did the pilot in April 1985," Betty would write later. "And it was a real treat to work with such pros. When you threw out a line, you had to brace yourself. because you knew it would be coming right back at you over the net and you'd better be ready."

In those days, such a condition was considered more or less beyond treatment. Allen and Betty were told right away that he didn't have long to live. The diagnosis was, in effect, a death sentence.

They shared the awful news with very few people. Allen wanted it that way, wanted to carry on as normally as possible. Not long after his surgery, from which he quickly recovered, he and Betty even appeared on an episode of *The Love Boat*, which featured Betty's old chum from *The Mary Tyler Moore Show*, Gavin MacLeod. Everyone seemed—and was—happy to reunite.

That fall, however, Allen slipped into a coma. He managed to pull out of it, but was not really the same afterwards. What relief he could find, he found on the California coast. The couple had been building a getaway home in the beachside community of Carmel, south of San Francisco. That, now, was their refuge. Allen got to sleep in the house only a couple of nights before he had to return to Los Angeles for care. He died on June 9, 1981, only five days before what would have been his 18th wedding anniversary with Betty. He was 63. Even though she knew Allen had been living on borrowed time for the previous several months, Betty was shattered. She had said many times, and would continue to say thereafter, "He was the love of my life."

Betty, who was 59 at the time of Allen's death, did her best to come to terms with her loss. "We had 18 wonderful years," she once said. "And you know, that's the lovely part of getting older. You've been through the joys and you've been through the grief, and you've lived through the cycles. You know you have to handle the grief, but you have enough confidence to know that somewhere in that deep well you will find something to help you through."

But it did seem as if a part of her had died with Allen Ludden. In the years to come, she didn't date all that much. The longing for companionship was still there—as she admitted to *The New York Times* not very long ago, "I see couples, and they'll be sitting there and all of a sudden one will put a hand over the other's. I miss that kind of personal contact"—but so far she has not seen fit to commit to marriage again.

ASPECTS OF BETTY'S PERSONAL STATE of mind—those having to do with loss and grief and aging—created an obvious but no less poignant subtext to Betty's next big project, *The Golden Girls*. Debuting on NBC in September 1985, the sitcom, like *The Mary Tyler Moore Show* before it, was groundbreaking. Whereas *MTM* had explored the life of a single woman pursuing her career unencumbered by a man, *Golden Girls* focused on four older women living in Miami, dealing in a refreshingly straightforward way with sudden and perhaps unwanted independence, with loneliness, with their social and even sex lives—all that. This unconventional concept was a surprising instant hit. A large part of the appeal was the obvious chemistry of the

VOICE LESSONS
Early on, Betty was concerned that her character, Rose, was the least well-defined of the four leads. It was not until director Jay Sandrich advised her to play Rose as a sweet, trusting sort, who "believes everything she is told and in her innocence, always takes the first meaning of every word," that Betty felt she had found the key to her character.

four principals—Betty played Rose Nylund; Rue McClanahan was Blanche Devereaux; Bea Arthur was Dorothy Zbornak; and Estelle Getty was Sophia Petrillo. Each actress would be nominated for Emmy Awards during the program's seven-season run and would win at least one; the show itself would twice be given the Emmy Award for Outstanding Comedy Series. Hardly done at age 90, the perennial nominee White had, by 2012, won seven Emmy Awards, daytime and nighttime varieties, for everything from being a deft supporting actress on *MTM* (1975 and '76), to being an engaging game show host on *Just Men!* (1983), to rocking the house as the host of *Saturday Night Live* (2010). She has also won three American Comedy Awards, including a Lifetime Achievement Award, has been inducted into the Television Hall of Fame and has been honored with a star on the Hollywood Walk of Fame, this last alongside Allen Ludden's.

The original plan with *Golden Girls* had been for Betty to portray the Southern belle Blanche, but then there were second thoughts. Blanche was to be a man-eater, and the producers feared that she would seem too much like Sue Ann. Betty was switched to the role of Rose, who was kind of a ditz—but not exactly. She wasn't clueless, but rather, as Betty explained, "terminally naïve. She's totally innocent." The character was jaw-droppingly literal-minded. "If you told her you could eat a horse," said Betty, "she would call the S.P.C.A."

Rather than appealing only to an expected older and largely female demographic, the show struck a chord with a wide range of viewers, thanks to the rich characterizations, which resisted stereotype at every turn. "These people proved you had the same sort of lust, the humor, the same everything that you've always had," Betty said. "The kids picked up on it." Yes, there were mature women and savvy kids in the audience, but in a real eye-opener at the time, the show also became a cult classic among gay men. It certainly helped that one of the key supporting characters in the first season was a homosexual housekeeper, but as Betty explained to *Parade* magazine, it was more elemental than that: "Gays love old ladies." Betty, who has always been open about her own tolerant views, was cheered by this latest addition to her still growing and more diverse fan base. "I don't care who anybody sleeps with," she said. "If a couple has been together all the time—and there are gay relationships that are more solid than some heterosexual ones—I think it's fine if they want to get married."

BETTY WAS, IN THIS PERIOD, EVOLVING into the public Betty who has, in recent years, wound up as one of America's best-loved celebrities, the whip smart and sly woman who is, in her seniority, as sharp as any youngster, as funny as any

PAUL DRINKWATER/NBC/GETTY (2)

other comic on the scene, as open-minded and generous and altogether lovely as anyone in the room. She's become the clever grandma every child would be happy and proud to acknowledge at the holiday table, and would steal away with for fun and games.

As she has become more and more famous, the at-home Betty has become a bigger part of her story, with her devotion to animals in particular getting such attention that she is known in some quarters—to her own delight—as "the animal lady." For decades, no issue has been closer to Betty's heart than animal welfare. As we've seen, she inherited her love of creatures great and small from her parents, Horace and Tess. She likes to joke that her mom and dad would probably have been happier if she had come into the world with four legs instead of two. As it was, they kept their home well stocked with all manner of critter. "They could come back from a walk with the dog, saying, 'Betty, he followed us home. Can we keep him?' " she recalled to *Parade*. "My parents had a cat named Toby who liked to sit on my crib. My mom always said that if Toby hadn't approved of the baby, I'd have gone straight back to the hospital."

Betty cheerfully refers to herself as an animal "nut," but also takes pains to point out that she's not part of the animal rights movement, with its sometimes fierce opposition to things like zoos. (She is extremely dedicated to well-run zoos, as we will soon see.) Betty says that her support stops well short of "animal rights and the political end of it." What she has focused on over the years is, she says simply, "animal welfare."

One of the chief beneficiaries of her activism has been the Morris Animal Foundation, with which she has been associated for more than 40 years. The Denver-based organization is primarily dedicated to finding cures and

A MATTER OF DEATH AND LIFE

In the show's second season, in an episode that explores the issue of death and how to live in its shadow, Rose suffers a severe throat spasm (above), has a near-death experience and decides to change her normally reserved ways and live a more fulfilled life. The premise is mined for laughs as her housemates find her new-found focus on self a tad annoying, but the episode is a telling example of the show's potent combination of humor, pathos—and, regularly, reality.

KEN HIVELY/LOS ANGELES TIMES/AP

treatments for health problems that affect companion animals, horses and wildlife. Many of their efforts involve pretty cutting-edge stuff, such as stem-cell research to help paralyzed dogs. But Betty has been an advocate for the simpler things, too, raising general awareness, staging a cancer walk for dogs and tacitly urging animal adoptions by her own example. In many ways, Betty is the face of the foundation, and she is no passive presence. A while back, she started thinking about the pain that animals suffer after they've had surgery, concluding that something should be done about it. "I said nobody was addressing pain in animals," she recalled. "They took care of the animals and all that, but they didn't think about the pain side of it." Betty suggested that Morris undertake a study to examine the most effective ways to alleviate this pain, and the foundation thought it was a terrific idea. There was, as there often is, however, one small problem. How would the project be funded? In the end, Betty came to her own rescue and supplied the seed money to get the study off the ground. "I had just gotten a commercial that was paying me too much money," she said wryly.

The other beneficiary of Betty's passion has been the Los Angeles Zoo. She has been a trustee of its parent organization since 1974, and the zoo is as near and dear to her heart as almost any other enterprise. A longtime Angelino, she remembers well when the place was an undistinguished little facility in Griffith Park. Now, it covers 133 acres, and Betty is well acquainted with just about every inch of it.

One of her delights in life is to visit the animals early in the morning in the company of keepers before the general public arrives. She fondly remembers one day when, during one of these special tours, she met Gita, an Asian elephant. As Betty explains in her book *Betty & Friends*, it was love at first sight. Gita would open her mouth to have her tongue slapped—something elephants enjoy beyond measure. "Gita was truly exceptional," Betty wrote. "I was amazed at her gentle disposition and human awareness/curiosity." About their relationship, which grew after that first morning, Betty said: "Whenever I got to walk with Gita, I was in heaven."

Betty's interactions with the zoo led to a friendship with the famous primate researcher Jane Goodall, and any number of other fine relationships with homo sapiens who feel as she does about the fellow animals with whom we share a planet. But Gita, who was regarded as the matriarch of the zoo, was a truly special kindred spirit. The elephant died in 2006 at the ripe old age of 48. Betty remembers Gita—and all the many animals who have come and gone in her life—fondly. Asked not long ago how she would like to be remembered, she didn't hesitate. "Probably for my animal work," she said. "The animal world has really come to the point where we realize what a major part of our lives they are, so that's how I'd like to be remembered."

And that is why, as we deal with Betty's golden years—during which animals have played an ever more important role—we spend a bit of time emphasizing this abiding passion. Many celebrities consider their careers a principal cause. With Betty, for many years now, it has been well down the list.

AN ABIDING PASSION
Not surprisingly, Betty's first book, published in 1983, was called *Betty White's Pet Love* and chronicled her love for animals. Opposite, she is joined at a party for the new book by Boomer, formerly the star of TV's *Here's Boomer*, an adventure series that ran for two seasons on NBC, about a lovable mixed-breed dog who travels the country helping those in need. Over the years, Betty has befriended many four-legged friends, but as she would write in *Betty & Friends* of her pachyderm pal above, "Yes, Gita, dear, you are still my very favorite of all."

GLOBE/ZUMA

Betty White's
PET•LOVE
How Pets Take Care of Us
Betty White with Thomas J. Watson

Golden Girl

DAVID MCGOUGH/DMI

Betty and Bea

During the first season of *The Golden Girls*, Betty and Bea Arthur (left, with Betty at *Night of 100 Stars*, a variety show in 1990 to benefit the Actors Fund, and opposite during an episode of *Golden Girls*) bonded over the common experience of coping with ailing mothers—Bea's mother, Bea Frankel, and Betty's mother, Tess, would both pass away within three weeks of one another. Bea also shared with Betty a successful past on television, having made a splash on *All in the Family* before starring in her own groundbreaking show, *Maude*, for six seasons. Bea's Dorothy on *Golden Girls* was a little like a more irascible version of Mary Tyler Moore's Mary Richards: the sane one in the ensemble who keeps the others in balance.

Dancing Fools (overleaf)

By the time *Golden Girls* reached its 100th episode, the show was a firmly established hit, allowing its stars to engage in ever zanier bits, like the dance sequence with Betty and Rue McClanahan on the following pages. Those two in particular often danced on the show, frequently in tap shoes.

ABC PHOTO ARCHIVES/GETTY

JOSEPH DEL VALLE/NBC/GETTY (3)

CBS/LANDOV

Skit Star

Betty became one of Johnny Carson's favorite *Tonight Show* guests, particularly if he had a skit for her to appear in with him, ideally one involving skimpy attire, like the one, opposite, in which Jane and Tarzan (Betty and Johnny) are now a quarreling couple on the verge of divorce. "When Johnny had an idea for a sketch," Betty would later write, "he'd call me to talk it down. I finally accused him of calling me whenever he wanted to take his clothes off. We did a lot of skits that were great fun." Betty described her many appearances on *The Carol Burnett Show*—she appears above with Steve Martin, left, and Tim Conway—as "marvelous, but not for the faint of heart, as everyone on the show was a multitalent."

AP

JOE HAMILTON PRODUCTIONS/EVERETT

Dysfunctional Family

Even before *Golden Girls* came along to ease Betty's pain over the loss of Allen Ludden, Betty's dear friend Carol Burnett was there, offering Betty work whenever she needed it. Betty had appeared in several of the "family" sketches on Carol's variety show, and when the family was spun off into a sitcom of its own, called *Mama's Family*, in 1983, Betty's character was written into the new show. Betty played Ellen, the rich, bitchy daughter of Vicki Lawrence's Mama (above, in pearls), who always stole the spotlight from her resentful sister, Eunice, played by Carol. Others in the cast included Ken Berry (above, middle) as Ellen's goofy brother, Vinton; Dorothy Lyman (above, second from left) as Vinton's oversexed wife, Naomi; and Allan Kayser (far left) as Eunice's screwup son, Bubba.

PAUL JENKINS

GLOBE/ZUMA

The Energizer Betty

While some performers might begin to think about slowing down in their 60s, Betty just kept humming along. In addition to *Golden Girls* and *Mama's Family*, the 1980s saw Betty continue her appearances on game shows—she was on 80 episodes of *The $25,000 Pyramid* during the decade—as well as her frequent guest spots on variety shows of every ilk, including an appearance in a salute to vaudeville with Donald O'Connor, above left, and Tony Randall that was part of the 1988 special, *Happy Birthday Bob* [Hope]—*50 Stars Salute Your 50 Years at NBC*. Betty was 66 at the time.

You Gotta Have Friends

Friends have always been enormously important to Betty and she has been blessed to have a great many close ones, including Lucille Ball, opposite, whom Betty first met in the earliest years of television. (One of Betty's first sitcoms in the '50s, *Date with the Angels*, was filmed at Desilu Studios, owned by Lucy and her husband Desi Arnaz, just a couple of soundstages away from where Lucy was recording the seminal *I Love Lucy*.) Not only did Betty and Lucy become friends, but their mothers did as well, and after Lucy's mother, DeDe, died, Lucy sent violets to Betty's mother, Tess, every year on DeDe's birthday.

KEVIN WINTER/DMI

GLOBE/ZUMA

In the Kitchen with Dinah

Another one of Betty's longtime friends was Dinah Shore, and Betty always loved going on any of the several iterations of her daytime talk show, as here in 1990, when she and Dinah baked some cookies together. Many years before, it had been an appearance by Burt Reynolds on Betty's show, *The Pet Set,* that had brought him to Dinah's attention and led to their well-publicized romance, which morphed in later years into a strong and enduring friendship. Their first public appearance together was at one of Betty and Allen's barbecues. Among Betty's treasured gifts is one of Dinah's accomplished oil paintings, this one of a beautiful seascape and inscribed, "To Betty and Allen with love, Dinah."

Funny Gals

In 1991, Betty was honored to appear with an unforgettable multi-generational all-star cast on *Funny Women of Television: A Museum of Television & Radio Tribute*. Spanning 40 years of television history, the show featured clips as well as live recollections from many of the iconic comediennes present. Top row from left: Jasmine Guy (representing the younger generation), producer Jack Haley Jr. and Justine Bateman (of *Family Ties* fame). Bottom row: Marlo Thomas, Tracey Ullman, Lily Tomlin, Carol Burnett, Mary Tyler Moore and Betty—causing mischief.

CHAPTER FOUR

EVERYBODY LOVES *BETTY*

AS THE 21ST CENTURY TRUNDLES ALONG, AMERICANS REVEL IN THEIR FAVORITE NONAGENARIAN, WHO SHOWS NO SIGNS OF SLOWING DOWN

"WE'RE HAVING SO MUCH FUN IT'S ILLEGAL, Betty White told *People* magazine. "It's nice to know you don't self-destruct." Actually, there were two more words: "It's nice to know you don't self-destruct *after 40*." She was, in fact, 63 at the time, and she was speaking of her gig on *Golden Girls*. In 2012, she turned 90, and a half-century after 40 she still showed no signs of self-destruction. If anything, she was more famous, more popular and making more money than ever. She has had a couple of TV programs, a big career as a pitchwoman (marked most recently by her hire as the face of Tide's new laundry detergent, renamed Vivid White and Bright), the occasional movie project and a sideline career as a host a and an always welcome guest. "What else do I have lined up?" she quipped to *TV Guide* one day about her late-in-life activity. "Well, it's only ... the morning!"

A PAIR OF LEGENDS

Betty's occasional boyfriend on *Hot in Cleveland* is played by comedy great Carl Reiner, who, like Betty, harkens back to the earliest days of television. Beginning in 1950, he was a writer and performer on the iconic *Your Show of Shows* with Sid Caesar, then played Dick Van Dyke's mercurial boss, Alan Brady, on *The Dick Van Dyke Show*. Carl was in the Army Entertainment Section during World War II with Betty's husband, Allen Ludden, whom he credits with getting him started in show business via a recommendation Allen made to another member of their unit, Maurice Evans. "Today, every so often," Betty writes in *If You Ask Me*, "Carl will say to me, 'Wouldn't Allen get a kick out of this if he were here—seeing us working together?' "

TV LAND/EVERETT

Hers has been, by any reckoning, an amazing run, made all the more amazing by the fact that it doesn't show any sign of flagging. It's tempting to view this late-in-life career surge as a renaissance, but the fact is that Betty never went away; if she had hotter and cooler periods, she certainly never disappeared.

In 1992 there was that ill-fated *Golden Girls* spinoff with three of the original four girls, and yes, true, it was short-lived. But, for Betty there began a spate of high-profile guest appearances on hit shows. A memorable turn on *Ally McBeal* gave a further glimpse of her devilish wit. (It involved suppositories, but for the sake of decorum we'll leave it at that.) She was nominated for Emmy Awards for her work on *Suddenly, Susan*; *The Practice*; *Yes, Dear*; and *My Name Is Earl*; she won for her send-up of a Betty White–like diva on *The John Larroquette Show*. From 2006 through 2009, when her character died of pancreatic cancer, she was featured on the daytime soap, *The Bold and the Beautiful*, and late-night audiences relished her frequent appearances on *The Late Late Show* with Craig Ferguson, where she might show up as a Girl Scout, a prison guard or the prospective President of the United States.

It might seem strange to compare her to Bill Murray, but their careers have followed parallel tracks in many ways. Long ago, both actors proved they could play serious as well as funny, and neither has ever lost that special comedic gift. As with Murray, Betty has gotten to the point in her life and career that all she has to do is show up, this gnomic white-haired lady, and we start to chuckle to ourselves. We know that almost anything she does in the next few minutes in that innocent, deadpan—and inimitable—way of hers is going to be hilarious.

Her particular signature has become playing against type and the constant pushing of boundaries. In the 1999 movie thriller *Lake Placid*, she plays a foul-mouthed widow with an unsavory connection to the giant crocodile that is terrorizing the lake. In the TV series *The Practice*, she is a cold-hearted blackmailer who eventually becomes, well, dangerously crazy.

And then there has been all of the sex stuff. Relying on the deep reservoir of goodwill she has built up, the ever-present, knowing twinkle in her eye and all of the license granted by age, she has realized that there's great good humor in playing bawdy—bawdier by half than even Sue Ann Nivens might have dreamed. Remember that shower scene she did with Hugh Jackman in a promo for Jay Leno's *Tonight Show*? Or that startling gag she delivered at the roast for her *Boston Legal* co-star William Shatner in 2006? "I once had sex with Bill Shatner," she said. "You should have seen him, sweating and grunting and so red in the face, and wheezing. Finally I said, 'Bill, you'd better hurry up and finish, in two

MARS CHOCOLATE/AP

PEERLESS PITCHWOMAN
Betty's career in commercials has come a long way from the days of *Hollywood on Television* in 1949, when she and co-host Al Jarvis had to perform numerous live advertisements—she once did 58 in a single day!—for their sponsors and a relatively small audience in the Los Angeles area. Now, an ad like her unforgettable Super Bowl spot, above, for Snickers—Nielsen ranked it as the best-liked ad of 2010—is seen by more than 100 million people.

minutes they're going to start the roast!' "

Could that have been our demure Betty?

Well, she hasn't been demure for a while—if she ever was.

She became water-cooler talk with almost every brief or recurring performance, even those in promos. Exhibit A might be that memorable Snickers ad during the 2010 Super Bowl. You wouldn't think that a commercial could move the needle much, but this one sure did. In it, Betty plays football along with fellow senior citizen Abe Vigoda against a horde of brutes before a Snickers bar transforms her into a much younger player. The sight of the trash-talking Betty (or her stunt double, at any rate) getting pounded into a muddy puddle and then rising triumphantly made millions of Super Bowl viewers wince—then burst out in cheers. The premise alone was funny, but the ad worked on so many levels, not least as a clever allusion to the sheer indomitability of this particular venerable, gutsy gal. The commercial wouldn't have been half as good with any other white-haired lady.

Maybe the stars were in alignment in 2010: Around the same time as the Super Bowl spot, a group led by a 29-year-old fan got together on Facebook to lobby for Betty to get a crack at hosting *Saturday Night Live*. What many of the online activists may not have known was that *SNL*'s executive producer, Lorne Michaels, had been trying for years to get Betty to come on the show. She had always begged off, to the point that Michaels simply had stopped asking. Even when a half-million Facebookers signed on to support her candidacy, she remained unmoved, telling her agent, "People have had such an overdose of me—they don't need me anymore!" Of course, she was wrong. There was no overdosing on Betty, and they wanted as much of her as they could get.

Michaels came up with an offer she couldn't refuse. He would assemble an all-star cast of female *SNL*ers—Tina Fey, Amy Poehler and Molly Shannon, among others—and would promote the episode as a special Mother's Day extravaganza. Betty relented, and once she was in, she was all the way in. She proceeded to turn up in nearly every skit that night, including one wildly ribald number involving "muffins." Don't ask. The musical guest that night was a large, male exception to the show's feminine theme because, as Michaels explained, "Jay-Z was excited about

DANA EDELSON/NBC/GETTY

the idea of working with Betty White."

Everybody loved Betty. Everybody still does.

KEVIN WINTER/GETTY

BETTY'S *SATURDAY Night Live* appearance won the show its best ratings since 2008 and beat even that evening's slate of prime-time shows. She won yet another Emmy for her *SNL* performance. No sooner had the fuss from all that died down than Betty delivered another buzzworthy guest appearance on *Community*—she had already been on *30 Rock* that season—recorded her voice work for what would become the hit feature-film adaptation of Dr. Seuss's *The Lorax* and also started appearing regularly in yet another television series, *Hot in Cleveland*, which almost immediately became a hit for TV Land. In this sitcom, she plays the caretaker of a home in the eponymous city who dishes out nasty wisecracks to the three fortyish women—Valerie Bertinelli, Jane Leeves and Wendie Malick—who have decided to rent the place. Betty is the spirit of the production, on the screen and on the set. "You can tell that Betty has always had a giggle in her heart," said Malick. "You can just tell she's approached her life with gratitude and joy."

She has, meanwhile, rallied others like her—and of her approximate age—for the NBC reality series *Betty's White's Off Their Rockers*, which she executive produces as well as stars in. The idea of

MUTUAL ADMIRATION

In the midst of receiving her own raft of awards (see following page), Betty occasionally has the opportunity to hand one out, and she was thrilled to join her pal Mary Tyler Moore (left, at right) in presenting the 2008 Emmy Award for Outstanding Comedy Series to Tina Fey of *30 Rock*. Two years later, Fey was able to return the favor by joining Betty for her appearance on *Saturday Night Live*, along with a gaggle of female former *SNL* stars, including (top, from left) Ana Gasteyer and Molly Shannon, who reprised their classic NPR-skewering skit, "Delicious Dish" with Betty.

REED SAXON/AP

MATT SAYLES/AP

DUFFY-MARIE ARNOULT/WIREIMAGE/GETTY

A LOAD OF HARDWARE

Betty's recent awards include (clockwise, from above) the Screen Actors Guild Lifetime Achievement Award, in 2010; the SAG award for Outstanding Performance by a Female Actor in a Comedy Series, for *Hot in Cleveland,* in 2012; and the Jane Goodall Institute Global Leadership Award for Lifetime Achievement, given by Jane Goodall herself in 2009, for Betty's tireless work on behalf of animals.

this hidden-camera show is that golden gals and guys prank (or punk) the younger generation. It is, of course, a hit.

BETTY WHITE JUST KEEPS SMILING, chuckling at her good fortune and her gradual elevation as an American icon—our democratic nation's beloved Queen Mum of Comedy. Even as her show business life has become increasingly frenetic on many fronts, her personal life has remained simple and straightforward. She has lived in the same home in the Brentwood section of Los Angeles for decades. It's a nice place, but hardly ostentatious. Even this late in life, she continues to drive herself most places. She has a fondness for Cadillacs and names them after birds. "Parakeet" might refer to a pet

PETE SOUZA/THE WHITE HOUSE/CORBIS

or a car. (Actually, with Betty, it's a car—she has declared that while she likes all animals, her favorites are four-legged.)

Though she is almost constantly at work on one book or another, she will probably not be issuing a *Betty White Diet Plan for Seniors* anytime soon. She likes meat, and supplements main courses with french fries most nights. It works for her.

As she hilariously disclosed during her *Saturday Night Live* opening monologue, technology is not something she pays much attention to. She really is the dyed-in-the-wool Luddite she painted herself as that night, when she noted the Facebook campaign that had led to her hire by *SNL*, then said she had to go investigate what this thing "Facebook" was, explaining that when she wanted "to connect with old friends, I need a Ouija board." Once she understood Facebook better, she concluded: "It sounds like a huge waste of time." But, she does now have a Twitter handle—not bad for someone who, when breaking into show business, figured radio was the only way. She made news during the election season when she expressed her support for President Obama, which led to an audience in the Oval Audience. After her visit to Washington, she dropped her own facetiously titled White Power presidential bid, which had been announced to great excitement on Ferguson's show.

Of course, there could be a groundswell, as there has been before with this cherished woman. Who among us could look at Betty White after all these years and not wonder, *What about 2016?*

What will she be up to then?

A WHITE IN THE WHITE HOUSE

While she has generally avoided politics for fear of alienating her fans, Betty came out in favor of Barack Obama in 2012, an endorsement that led to a White House visit with the President, above, in June, as well as discussion among Democrats about having Betty speak at their convention to answer the appearance by earlier LIFE Icon Clint Eastwood at the Republican confab.

Everybody Loves Betty

Betty the Vamp

Betty has always done whatever it takes to get a laugh, so she was more than willing to lounge in luxury for this poolside shoot with several selected beefcake models. Of course, Betty always makes the most of her opportunities—originally shot for a story on Betty in *Entertainment Weekly*, this picture would end up appearing in her *2011 Betty White Calendar*, with proceeds benefitting her favorite charity, the Morris Animal Foundation. Not surprisingly, there was also some fur to go with all the skin in the calendar: several months commemorated by shots of Betty with her favorite pets.

MICHAEL ELINS/OUTLINE/CORBIS

MPTVIMAGES

TV LAND/EVERETT

Chemistry Set

"On *Hot in Cleveland,* when we'd all been cast and come together for our first table read, we all simply fell in love," Betty writes in *If You Ask Me*. "It was that instant rapport.... We all just love to laugh." As with *The Golden Girls*, Betty was surrounded by pros, including (right, left to right) Jane Leeves, who charmed the nation for 11 seasons as Daphne Moon on *Frasier*, Wendie Malick, whose stints on *Dream On* and *Just Shoot Me!* had made her a star—she also appeared on *Frasier* in the show's final season as the character who ends up marrying Frasier's father, Marty—and Valerie Bertinelli, who starred as a teenager on *One Day at a Time* and later was a regular on *Touched by an Angel*. A number of Betty's old friends have stopped by the show to add to the hilarity, including Mary Tyler Moore, above, who shares a laugh with Betty during a memorable jailhouse scene. It is Betty's third successful ensemble cast. Coincidence? Not by a long shot.

CLIFF OWEN/AP

Ranger Betty

Betty has often credited her parents, Horace and Tess, as the source of her love for animals. But they also instilled in her a passion for nature and the great outdoors in general. On the last day of school, her parents would often pick her up at Beverly Hills High School—her dad in his well-worn forest ranger hat—and off the family would head, to the High Sierras or Yellowstone National Park, where they would go for days, she says, "without seeing another two-legged soul." That experience inspired a childhood dream to be a Forest Ranger. Well, it took her a while, but in 2010, at a special ceremony held by the U.S. Forest Service at Washington's Kennedy Center for the Performing Arts, Betty finally got her wish as she was designated an honorary Forest Ranger (above) at the age of 88. In her acceptance speech, Betty said that her parents "would be more proud of this than any other award I have won." Betty is particularly pleased that the U.S. Forest Service, which once prohibited women from being rangers, now has women comprising one third of its work force.

Rock On, Betty

Betty's latest project is *Betty White's Off Their Rockers*, an updated version of the old *Candid Camera*, with seniors doing the punking of their unwitting, much younger marks and Betty in the role of host, Allen Funt. The first episdode of the show was broadcast on January 16, 2012, deliberately timed to help celebrate Betty's 90th birthday the next day. It returned for 11 more episodes in April and May, received more than respectable ratings and has been renewed for the 2012–13 television season. "It's the reverse psychology of the 'poor old seniors,'" Betty says of the show. "We've got a sense of humor too, warped as it may be." Celebrity guests have included *The Love Boat's* Ted Lange, 64, game show host Wink Martindale, 77, and Batman, himself, Adam West, 83. Two ongoing successful shows in her 90s? Just another milestone for Betty.

KERRY HAYES/WALT DISNEY STUDIOS MOTION PICTURES/EVERETT

New Friends

Every year brings Betty new fans and new friends. In 2009, she starred with Sandra Bullock and Ryan Reynolds in *The Proposal*, playing a sweet but—surprise, surprise—mischievous grandmother. Both of the movie's leads now count themselves as fans; the three made an hilarious mock promotional spot for the film that became a huge hit on the website *Funny or Die* and included Betty calling Ryan "an ab-crunching jackass." Of working with Betty, Sandra declared, "You have to play the straight guy. There's no way you're going to match her." Betty would later write of her co-star: "What a joy it was to work with Sandra. Here's this big movie star and there wasn't anything "movie star" about her. We became great and dear friends. Still are. The same goes for Ryan Reynolds."

FRED PROUSER/REUTERS

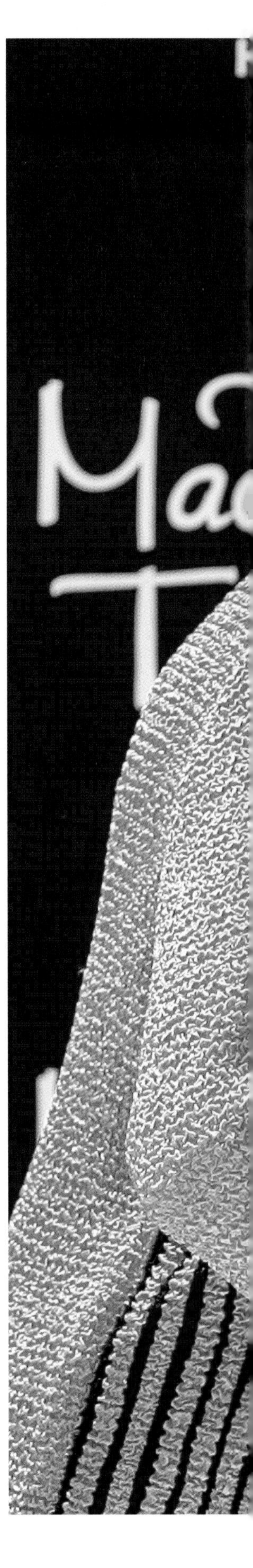

Still a Trouper

Betty's life keeps circling back on itself, with reunions and reprises alternating regularly with new experiences, new friends, new connections. When the American Academy of Television Arts & Sciences honored Betty in 2008 for her 60 years in television, Ed Asner, Betty's pal and castmate on *The Mary Tyler Moore Show*, was there to help celebrate the event, above. Four years later, Ed guest starred on *Hot in Cleveland* with Betty, playing a former lover, destined to get his comeuppance from Betty's character whom he had spurned years earlier. Ed would later joke to *Parade* magazine, "She has become an American institution. I have to bend my knee every time I run into her and I'm getting tired of it!"

Of course, few honors bespeak the status of "American institution" as much as being celebrated with your own look-alike in Madame Tussauds Hollywood wax museum. Betty received the honor in June 2012, one of several such honors marking her 90th birthday. Ever the trouper, Betty (opposite, getting acquainted with her doppelganger) found ample humor in the situation. "I think they did a wonderful job," she said. "I'm really amazed. I'm so impressed." Her only complaint? "She won't look at me. I keep talking to her, but she won't turn her head."

BRET HARTMAN/REUTERS

At Home

Even in her younger days, Betty was a homebody, who preferred the company of animals to the glitzy Hollywood glamour set. At right, she relaxes with the basics: a dog at her feet, a portait of Allen Ludden on the table beside the couch, and, just out of view, a dining room table that contains piles and piles of material relating to her many projects. As she writes in *If You Ask Me*, "What about my potential dinner guests? With no place to serve them, we wind up with cocktails and hors d'oeuvres in the den, then we go out to eat. I am not what might be called one of the world's greatest hostesses." One suspects that her guests never complain, content, perhaps, to simply revel in Betty's active and upbeat approach to life. "If one is lucky enough to be blessed with good health," she writes, "growing older shouldn't be something to complain about. It's not a surprise, we knew it was coming—make the most of it. So you may not be as fast on your feet, and the image in the mirror may be a little disappointing, but if you are still functioning, and not in pain, gratitude should be the name of the game."

MARK SENNET

CHRIS PIZZELLO/AP

Our National Treasure

The hugs, proffered by Betty's *Hot in Cleveland* castmates (from left) Valerie Bertinelli, Wendie Malick and Jane Leeves, are at the 2012 People's Choice Awards, where the show was honored as the nation's favorite cable TV comedy. The sentiment, writ large in bright lights, is forever.